CW01183222

WORLD of Sheepy

Sheepy and The Riddle of the Occurrence

by Henrietta Williams

Illustrated by Richard Berner

Copyright © 2016 Henrietta Williams
Illustrations © Henrietta Williams & World of Sheepy

The moral right of the author has been asserted.

Apart from any fair dealing for the purposes of research or private study, or criticism or review, as permitted under the Copyright, Designs and Patents Act 1988, this publication may only be reproduced, stored or transmitted, in any form or by any means, with the prior permission in writing of the publishers, or in the case of reprographic reproduction in accordance with the terms of licences issued by the Copyright Licensing Agency. Enquiries concerning reproduction outside those terms should be sent to the publishers.

This is a work of fiction. Names, characters, businesses, places, events and incidents are either the products of the author's imagination or used in a fictitious manner. Any resemblance to actual persons, living or dead, or actual events is purely coincidental.

Matador
9 Priory Business Park,
Wistow Road, Kibworth Beauchamp,
Leicestershire. LE8 0RX
Tel: 0116 279 2299
Email: books@troubador.co.uk
Web: www.troubador.co.uk/matador
Twitter: @matadorbooks

ISBN 978 1785890 956

British Library Cataloguing in Publication Data.
A catalogue record for this book is available from the British Library.

Printed and bound in Malta by Gutenberg Press Ltd
Typeset by Troubador Publishing Ltd, Leicester, UK

Matador is an imprint of Troubador Publishing Ltd

To Alex, Nick, Jamie and Josh

An Introduction

High on a hill, overlooking fields dotted with white and seas patched with blue, can be found a strange and magical world inhabited by the strangest and most magical creatures that you could ever hope to clap eyes upon.

However, clapping eyes aside, it is my sincere and heartfelt duty to tell you that if you are considering searching for this mystical land, then please STOP.

Save yourself the trouble as not only will you never catch a twinkling glimpse but you'll also never hear, smell or touch it because, to put it bluntly, it does not wish to be found.

Of course, the inhabitants would love to be found. The dwellers on the hill would give their ears and their cheeks to be found. They wouldn't think twice about adding fingers, toes and even their most important hats to be found.

Just for the tiniest of peeps or for the merest of journal mentions, written, perhaps, as such:

> SUNDAY 18th OCTOBER
> Went for a nice walk today.
> Thought i saw something in the stump of a tree.
> Not sure what it was.
> Oh well.
> Had fish for tea.

It is the world that does not wish to be discovered. And so it never has been, never will be, and, quite possibly, never could be. Unless by accident or perhaps by reading the pages of this book.

Yes, that's quite possibly the only way that the magical little world on the hill could ever succumb to the tiniest of eye-claps and perhaps the slightest suggestion of a knee-knock.

So, my brave and curious travellers, this is your only chance to peer inside, under and around the world on the hill. And if you have the indulgence to pass on what you have discovered, please let it never be said that I was the one who told you so.

I bid you good day.

Sheepy

As the warmth of the glowing ball in the sky trickled through the carefully crafted canopy above, a creature as fluffy as a cloud and as likeable as eggnog dozed against the base of a tree stump.

It had been a longish doze and just about sufficient to place the creature at around ninety per cent of its full capacity, which was much more than enough to get it through the day with or without additional sustenance.

Sustenance for the creature could usually be found in the guise of cappers, flickjabs and kettle snips although, due to the season of the month, thumb mites were probably much more in evidence amongst the scrabblings of the forest floor.

The creature yawned a slow and comfortable yawn; sighed a slow and comfortable sigh, before rolling on to one side and shifting itself with the aid of a bony, twig-like elbow.

"SHEEPY!"

Now, never let it be said that anger entered the creature's fluffy white head or anything as strong as irritation. However, it was with the tiniest modicum of consternation that it turned to see the owner of the shout that had shattered the mid-morning ambience into the smallest of irretrievable pieces.

"SHEEPY!"

Again, the owner of the shout succeeded in further raising the fires of Bigatron by blustering and lurching with no regard for anything other than its own personal agenda of loudness.

Sheepy, the fluffy white creature who had been calmly resting and rejuvenating to reach a nearly maximum capacity of ninety per cent, got to his skinny pencil-like legs and held up his twig-like arm in order to announce his presence to the owner of the shouty voice.

"Ah, there you are, Sheepy. We've been looking everywhere for you. What have you been doing? You're covered in thumb mite husks and smeared with ointment," said Mr Shouty.

"Yes," said Sheepy. "It would appear to be so."

"Well then. Dust yourself off and scribble scrabble to the glade post-haste. There's been an occurrence and all dwellers are required to provide some level of listening and possible head-nodding."

Sheepy got to his feet and picked up his bag before slinging it over his shoulders and following the shouter, who had already started stomping off in the direction of the glade.

"I say, careful, Sheepy old boy. I'm trying to nibble on a numbscrap here and you're coagulating my mouth mess," said a voice from over Sheepy's shoulder.

"Sorry, Mouse," said Sheepy, "we've been summoned."

"Mmm, yes," said Mouse from inside Sheepy's bag, "mmm, yes, mmm, numbscraps."

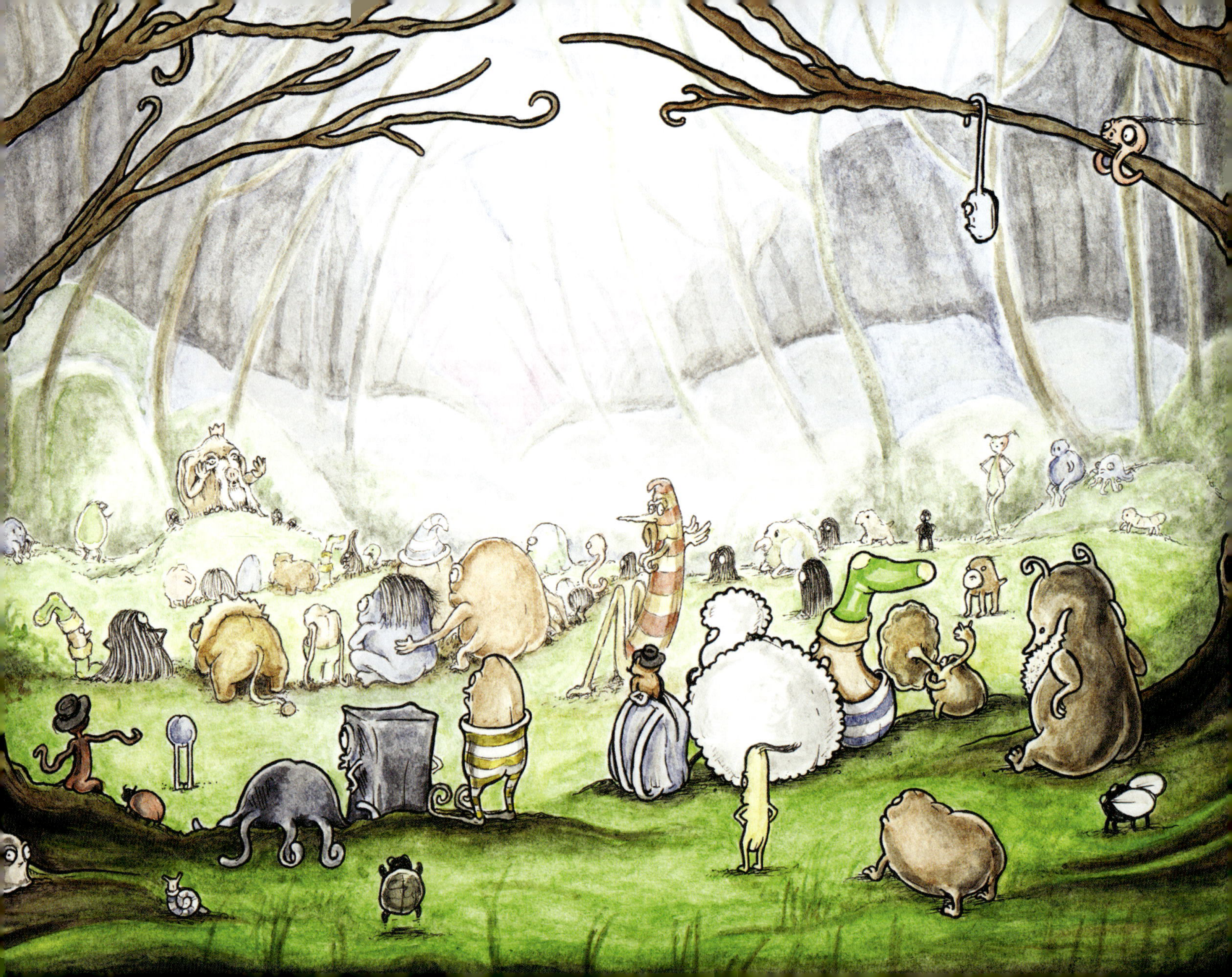

The Glade

As far as glades go, the one that was at the centre of Sheepy's world was pretty darn comfortable. There was enough moss to bounce a badger, plenty of wood chip for recreation and lots of surrounding trees for protection from goodness only knows what.

On this particular occasion the glade was packed full to the gills with all manner of nymph, nut and noodle, which made searching for a well-considered spot quite out of the question and quite in keeping with Sheepy's philosophy of sit and be satisfied.

"Any news of speakers, Sheepy?" Mouse asked, having just that second swallowed his final gulp of coagulated mouth mess.

"Not yet Mouse, nothing to report."

Sheepy wiggled his white fluffy bottom to gain further purchase on a mossy clump before shimmying his bag from his shoulders and allowing it to fall to the soft ground with a light flump.

"Steady on squire," growled Mouse as he unzipped the bag and poked his moustachioed head out of the top.

"Sorry Mouse," mumbled Sheepy as he gazed upon the ever increasing crowd that was doing its level best to accommodate every available crook and nook.

"Quite all right old boy," winked Mouse as he adjusted his bow tie and sat on the bag alongside his fluffy white companion.

"Oh look, there's Sox," said Sheepy as a rotund little creature with boggle-eyes and a sock-shaped head appeared from behind a kneeling pipsqueak.

"Sheepy. Mouse. Good day to you both," said Sox as he dusted down his striped trouser leggings and scratched his elongated foot-shaped head.

"Sox old boy," smiled Mouse whilst teasing his moustache and adjusting his hat, "good to see you."

"Yes Sox," said Sheepy, still watching the crowd for signs of an occurrence, "good to see you too."

Sox settled down, leaving his bow neatly balanced between half-cocked and ready for action.

"Any news of the occurrence yet?" whispered Sox, not wishing to appear too out of touch with proceedings.

"Nothing yet Sox. We just got here ourselves. Still waiting for it." Mouse touched his nose and winked at Sox, which made Sox feel a little more at ease to be in the company of a moustachioed nose-toucher.

Just then a flag was raised to its full extent and a bugler held a severed acorn aloft and started to bugle.

The resulting noise was something significantly louder than a hat pin dropping onto a fridge magnet and definitely quieter than a wolf howling at the moon after losing its wife and family.

Sheepy, Mouse and Sox rose to their feet as did the rest of the glade, including the pipsqueaks.

News of an Occurrence

As the acorn fanfare came to a halt, a hushed silence fell over the glade as a rather fierce-looking creature with thick limbs and a wizened face was carried on to a raised mound of earth by two small, yet incredibly strong, mites.

"Ahem," growled the creature as it was placed at its superior vantage point.

"It's the chief," whispered Sheepy.

The crowd held their breath and waited in cautious anticipation as the chief raised himself still further upon his tiptoes, opened his mouth and closed his eyes.

For the next five or so minutes the chief held his pose and the crowd held their own. Not a sound was to be heard and not even the slightest suggestion of a song thrush dared to whisper whilst the traditional glade ceremony took place.

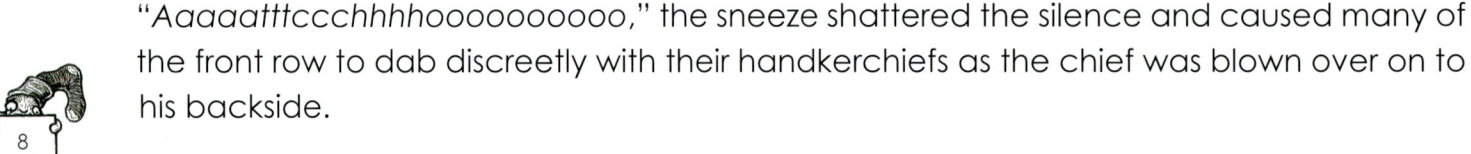

"*Aaaaatttccchhhhoooooooooo*," the sneeze shattered the silence and caused many of the front row to dab discreetly with their handkerchiefs as the chief was blown over on to his backside.

"Impressive," said Sox.

"Indeed," whispered Mouse.

"Can we talk now?" asked Sheepy.

"You can talk now!" shouted the chief, wiping his nose and placing his bottom on a throne that had been swiftly positioned to prevent his posterior from any further earth encounters.

"Oh good," said Sheepy, "what shall we talk about?"

"That's enough talking!" shouted the chief, raising his bottom back off the throne.

"Bum," said Sheepy.

"Sshh," whispered Sox.

"It has come to my attention," continued the chief as the crowd listened in silence, "that there's been an occurrence."

A collective noise of head-nodding and overt listening took place for around thirty seconds prior to the chief continuing.

"Hmmm, yes, quite," said the chief before he held his hand aloft. "Bring forth the occurrence!"

A glade council member, who could only be described as having the face of a fish and the body of an avocado, rolled his way towards the chief's throne but became stuck on a particularly gnarled and knotted twig.

"Urrm, a little help?" he requested politely.

After a bit of a heave-ho from the mites, the council member manoeuvred himself closer to the chief and presented him with a scrumpled piece of white paper.

A deeper hush fell upon the crowd as they watched the chief unfold and unfold and, yet again, unfold the paper scrumple until it was entirely covering the throne, the council member, the chief, the mites and the mound of earth.

"This!" cried the chief from under the unfolded piece of paper, "Is the occurrence!"

Everyone nodded and listened for further updates.

"It's very big and slightly soft of touch but other than that there are no clues."

Sheepy narrowed his eyes and digested the information thoughtfully and not without a smidgen of fearful curiosity.

"Now, I want you all to have a good look at it and then come up with some jolly good answers pertaining to what on earth it is and what on earth we should jolly well do with it."

Further head-nodding and even back-scratching ensued as the paper was refolded into a moveable size and wobbled away by the fish fruit council member.

"Now, I'll pass you over to the remaining members of the glade council to continue with today's proceedings. Good day!"

The entire glade dropped to their knees and in unison sang, "Good day to you great and honourable chieftain that is wise and a little bit scary but not without charm and a touch of a feathered chick, which has not yet left the nest."

Again, as one, the crowd rose as the chief left the mound of earth and was replaced by a council member who proceeded to cough and attempt to gain a measure of order and decorum as the crowd bleated, cried and guffawed at the news of the occurrence.

"Oh, before I forget." The crowd immediately dropped back to the floor as the chief retook the mound. "The occurrence will be tied to the Seventh Stump of Ancient Bewilderment if you need to get a closer look in order to get me some answers pertaining to its origin etc. etc."

"Good day, again," added the chief as he left the mound for the second time in two minutes.

"Good day to you, for the second time, great and honourable chieftain that is wise and a little bit scary but not without charm and a touch of a feathered chick, which has not yet left the nest."

"Well then, if it's answers he wants then it's answers he shall have and I don't mind telling you…"

Sox's speech on answers was interrupted by a whizz of breeze and flurry of leaves as an umbrella carrying a worm-like creature came to a smooth stop right in front of him.

Bob!

"Like, hey everyone, what's the news?"

"Hi Bob," said everyone.

Bob flopped his errant hair back over the top of his smooth green head and carefully folded his surf umbrella until it was no longer visible to the naked, or even the clothed eye.

"Soooo?" said Bob.

"Were you not present for the news of the occurrence?" asked Mouse, twisting both ends of his moustache into needle-sharp points.

"Urm, kinda but I was also doing a little bit of sleeping," whispered Bob.

"Sleeping!" cried Mouse, "At a glade meeting!"

"Shhhh, Mouse. Not loudly. Please, not loudly," hushed Bob.

"Sleeping," whispered Mouse, "at a glade meeting!"

"Yesssss," hissed Bob as a council member walked past, "what was the occurrence?"

After a quick recap of the glade meeting, purely for the benefit of sleepy Bob, Mouse climbed into Sheepy's bag and gave a quick glance of consternation before zipping himself in with no further comment.

"To the Circle of Ancient Bewilderment!" cried Sox.

"The what?" whispered Bob to Sheepy.

"Don't worry, Bob," said Sheepy, "we're going to visit the occurrence."

"Oh, the occurrence," nodded Bob, thoughtfully.

The Circle of Ancient Bewilderment

The Seventh Stump of Ancient Bewilderment had long been known as such, purely because no one actually could remember what had happened to the other six stumps.

As far as stumps go, it was not entirely bereft of character but couldn't exactly be called unique.

Moss – tick.

Knotholes – tick.

Bark on – tick.

Bark off – tick.

You get the picture.

In fact, the only remarkable quality of the stump was to be found within its name.

And as no one knew why it had been termed the Seventh Stump of Ancient Bewilderment it had continued to grow in mystery value until it was right up there with the Hole of Doom, the Nook of Plenty and even, in certain circles, the glade itself.

When Sheepy, Sox, Bob and Mouse arrived at the Seventh Stump of Ancient Bewilderment it was surrounded by pips, mites and buzzy creatures, the quantities of which had only ever been seen before at a hazelnut benefit dance.

Thankfully, as the aforementioned creatures were so small, Sheepy had no problem whatsoever in seeing the scrumpled piece of occurrence that was tied to the Seventh Stump of Ancient Bewilderment.

"Mouse," said Sheepy, "you might want to take a peep at this."

Mouse poked his head out of the bag and peeped over Sheepy's shoulder.

"Interesting, most interesting," considered Mouse as he twisted and twirled his facial fluff.

"Yes," agreed Sheepy.

"Mmmm," agreed Sox.

"Gnnnnooooorrr," snored Bob from within a fold of his umbrella.

"So, what kind of answers do you think we might be, urm, sort of, like, are there, what?" mumbled Sox as he looked up at Mouse, who was still twiddling and pondering to great aplomb.

"Well," said Mouse, without taking his gaze from the tied occurrence, "it looks to me like…"

"BAM!"

Out of nowhere a young nymph-like creature with crooked ears, steely eyes and an assured confidence that's never to be underestimated, slapped Sheepy on the back causing Mouse to jolt forward and lose his train of thought as well as his bus of consideration.

"Oh hello, Martha," said Sheepy.

"So, got any answers for the chief yet boys?"

"Well, I…" began Mouse.

"I'll be finding out so many answers that the chief will cover me in jellied jewels and shiny scraps until I'm yellow in the face with praise and reward!" Martha slapped her cotton-covered thigh and did a little jig before sitting down cross-legged on an opportune stool of fungus.

After a pertinent time of quiet reflection, Sox cleared his throat.

"So then, Martha," began Sox, "how are you thinking of approaching the answers in question?"

Martha sprang to her feet and grabbed Sox by the shoulders causing his sock-shaped head to quiver like a springy doorstopper.

"Why, with an adventure of course!" cried Martha as she jigged and thigh-slapped in a circle before finally sitting back on to the fungus stool with a gleam in her eye that was about as shiny as a new tooth.

"An adventure, Martha," smiled Sheepy, "that sounds exciting."

"Oh yes, an adventure. An exciting adventure. A super-duper exciting answer-finding adventure!" Martha's eyes continued to shimmer and shine like polished acorns as she stared at the tied occurrence with her legs crossed and her arms folded.

"What do you think, Mouse?" asked Sheepy over his shoulder. "Do you think we'll find some answers on an adventure?"

Everyone, except Bob, turned and stared upwards at Mouse and waited in anticipation.

Mouse pursed his lips and savoured the moment.

"Hmm," he pursed a bit more, "an adventure," a tiny bit more, "why not, eh?" and he relaxed.

"Woohoo!" yelled Martha leaping from her fungus seat and spinning Sox around by his bow.

"How exciting," said Sheepy, rubbing his paws together and raising his non-existent eyebrows to their full kilter.

"Ha ha!" cried Mouse, "This is what it's all about, eh Sheepy!"

"It certainly is Mouse," smiled Sheepy, "it certainly is."

"Hey, did I miss anything?" mumbled Bob as he unfolded himself like a newborn crocus.

"We're going on an adventure Bob," said Sheepy. "To find some answers for the chief."

"Ooohhh, an adventure, cool," Bob nodded as his flop of hair fell over his eyes preventing him from seeing and also preventing anyone else from noticing his slightly bewildered expression.

"Wait," cried Mouse, "let me take one long and lingering look at the occurrence before we go."

Everyone shuffled over to the occurrence in order to take one long and lingering look.

"Well, well, well," said Mouse, very, very slowly. "It looks like this little ditty may be a tad harder to explain than first anticipated."

With that, Mouse scribbled down the occurrence's particulars on a scrap of tree skin, zipped up Sheepy's backpack and said no more about it.

"Come on," said Sheepy to no one in particular, "let's go and have an adventure."

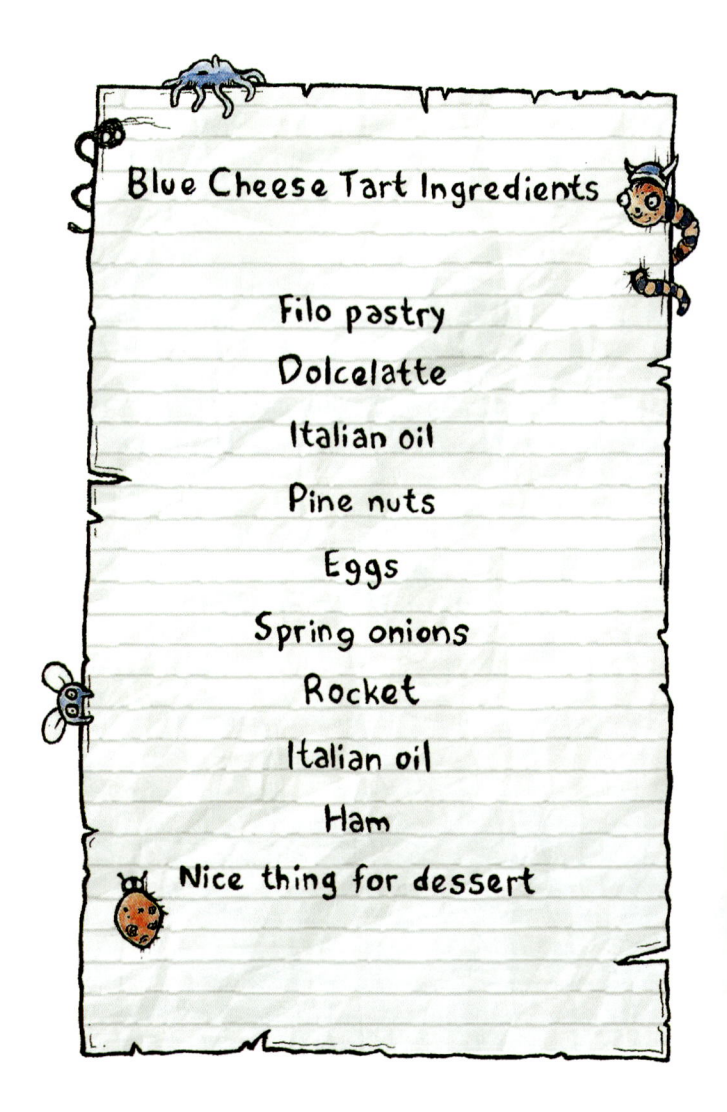

Blue Cheese Tart Ingredients

Filo pastry
Dolcelatte
Italian oil
Pine nuts
Eggs
Spring onions
Rocket
Italian oil
Ham
Nice thing for dessert

The Start of An Adventure

As all good adventures start with a visit to a shop so did this one and it wasn't long before Sheepy, Sox, Martha, Bob and Mouse, who was still zipped up in Sheepy's bag, were standing in front of a wooden counter with the sound of a bell still echoing sharply in their ears.

"Hello, hello, hello," called the shopkeeper from out the back, "won't keep you a moment."

Martha had already started examining a selection of dangerous looking beetles, which were safely placed behind reinforced glass, when there was a loud splash whereupon the shopkeeper appeared.

The shopkeeper was dressed in rather dandy fashion for the time of year and, although he was dripping wet from top to tail, he still managed to carry off a sniff of tailored finery that would have been more befitting a double-breasted lounge bar.

"Now, what can I do for you fine fellows?" beamed the shopkeeper, rubbing his fins together.

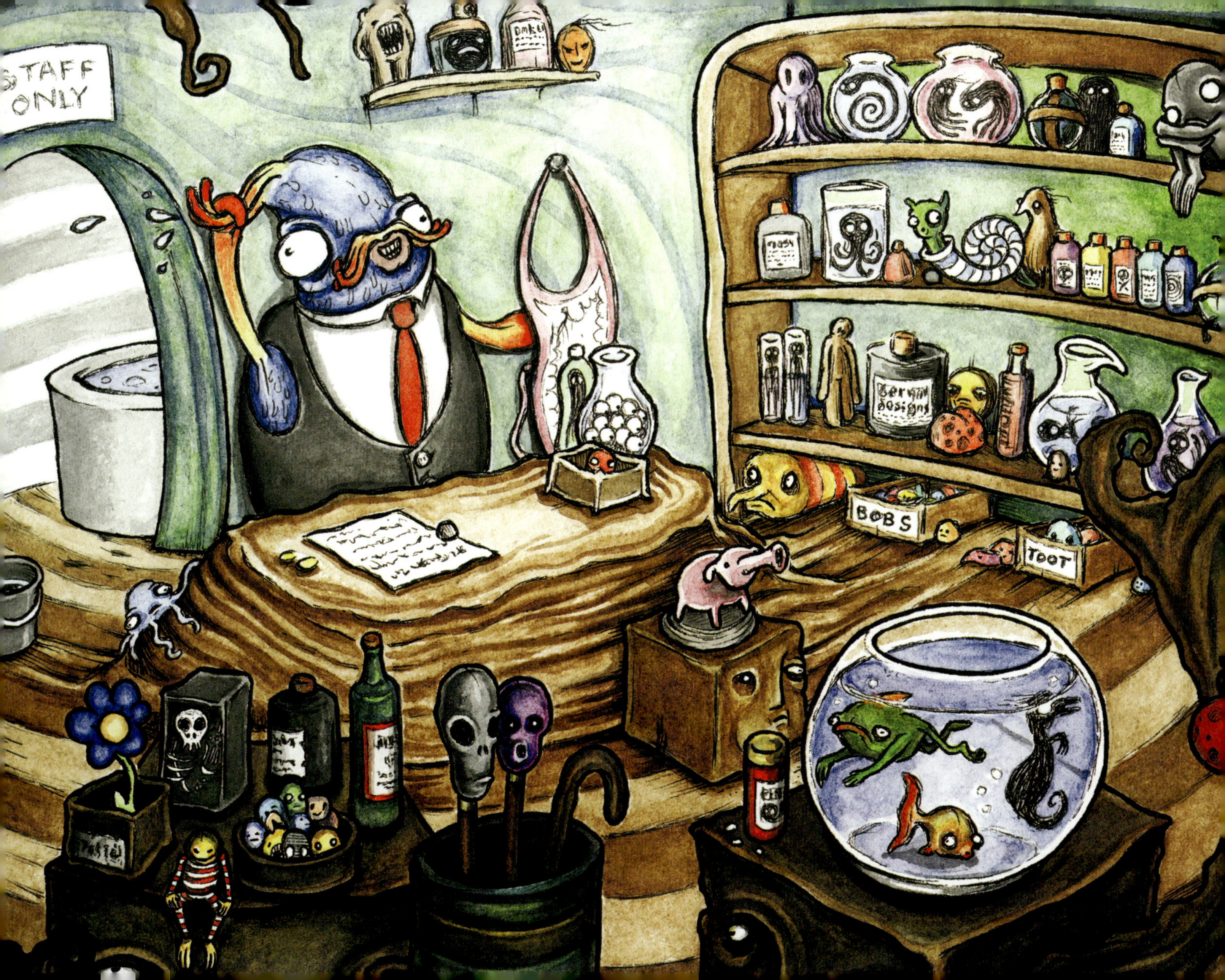
STAFF
ONLY
BOBS
TOOT

Martha shot him a glance worthy of a triple crown for excellence at a dart throwing competition, however, the shopkeeper continued unabated.

"We've got a wonderful assortment of bits and bobs today as well as quite the boxful of toot and nonsense," the shopkeeper rubbed his fins on his apron and flapped his gills more than enough times to be disconcerting.

There was a length of silence before, finally, Sox piped up.

"Urm, yes, we're going on an adventure and need some, ah, equipment."

Sheepy patted Sox on the back and waited patiently for the shopkeeper's reply.

"Oh now, an adventure is it? Well then, let me see," said the shopkeeper before promptly vanishing out the back where a lot of splashing could be heard and the occasional gulp.

"Nice fella," whispered Bob.

"Mmmm, lovely," agreed Sheepy.

"Yup," nodded Sox.

Martha said nothing, having turned her attention to an antiquated collection of throwing stars, which had been placed high up on the shop ceiling, safely out of the reach of nippers and pips.

"So then, what's it to be, my adventurous chums?" The shopkeeper was, again, dripping wet and seemed to have some kind of green algae hanging from his left gill.

"Urm, how about lots of bits, plenty of bobs and a little bit of nonsense?" asked Sheepy.

"No toot?" The shopkeeper cocked his large almond-shaped head on one side and allowed a singular bubble to escape from the corner of his thin-lipped mouth.

"No toot, thank you," affirmed Sheepy after receiving an affirmative nod from Sox.

"Right you are then," growled the shopkeeper, causing even Bob to look slightly affronted.

Outside the shop, Sheepy, Bob, Sox and Martha looked in the large brown leaf bag and mulled over their newfound possessions. There were certainly plenty of bits and bobs however; a small green leaf covering the nonsense looked less than encouraging.

"Knew we shouldn't have started an adventure at a shop," spat Martha, leaving a rather mucky residue all over an ill-fated dandelion.

"Oh well," said Sheepy taking off his backpack, "at least we've got plenty of bits and bobs to keep us going."

"Yes, but the nonsense!" Martha cried, rubbing her foot into the ground.

Sheepy unzipped his backpack and placed the large brown leaf bag containing the bits, bobs and nonsense inside.

"All tickity boo, Sheepy?" said Mouse.

"Oh yes Mouse, as tickity boo as can be expected," said Sheepy.

"Right you are. Mum's the word eh?" said Mouse, tapping his nose and nodding conspiratorially.

"How are you coming along with the occurrence, Mouse?" called out Sox.

"Never better Sox, never better," said Mouse, "I think it needs to be rearranged in order to create an answer."

With that, Sheepy zipped up his bag and slung it over his shoulders.

"Right then, let's do this!" shouted Martha, leaping in the air and slapping Sox around the head.

"Yeah, come on!" cried Sox, quite overcome with enthusiasm.

"Do what and the what now?" asked Bob, who had been enthusiastically contemplating another nap.

"Adventure, Bob. *Ad-ven-ture!*" spelled out Martha.

"Adventure, Bob!" concurred Sox.

"This way!" Martha yelled and immediately set off without further thought.

"Yeah!" cried Sox.

"Why not?" smiled Sheepy, "Come on Bob, let's have an adventure."

"A what?" said Bob.

A Twisty Turny Path

The path that Martha had spotted led up and around behind the shop before twisting and turning like a meandering uphill river. Leaves, sticks, bracken and plenty of loose soil somewhat hampered the speed of the adventurers, however, it did nothing to soak their spirits or even partially dampen them.

Martha was a born leader and although she had no idea where she was going or what she was looking for, she led from the front with all the confidence of a badger in a fistfight.

After a fair old while, which could have been an hour or perhaps a few minutes, Martha paused and raised her hand as if she were testing the breeze for tickles.

"Stop!" she cried, still with hand raised aloft.

Sheepy and Sox stopped walking whilst Bob slid his umbrella smoothly to rest by Sheepy's side.

"Look!" said Martha, changing her outstretched arm from halt to point.

There, just ahead, was a carved wooden bridge.

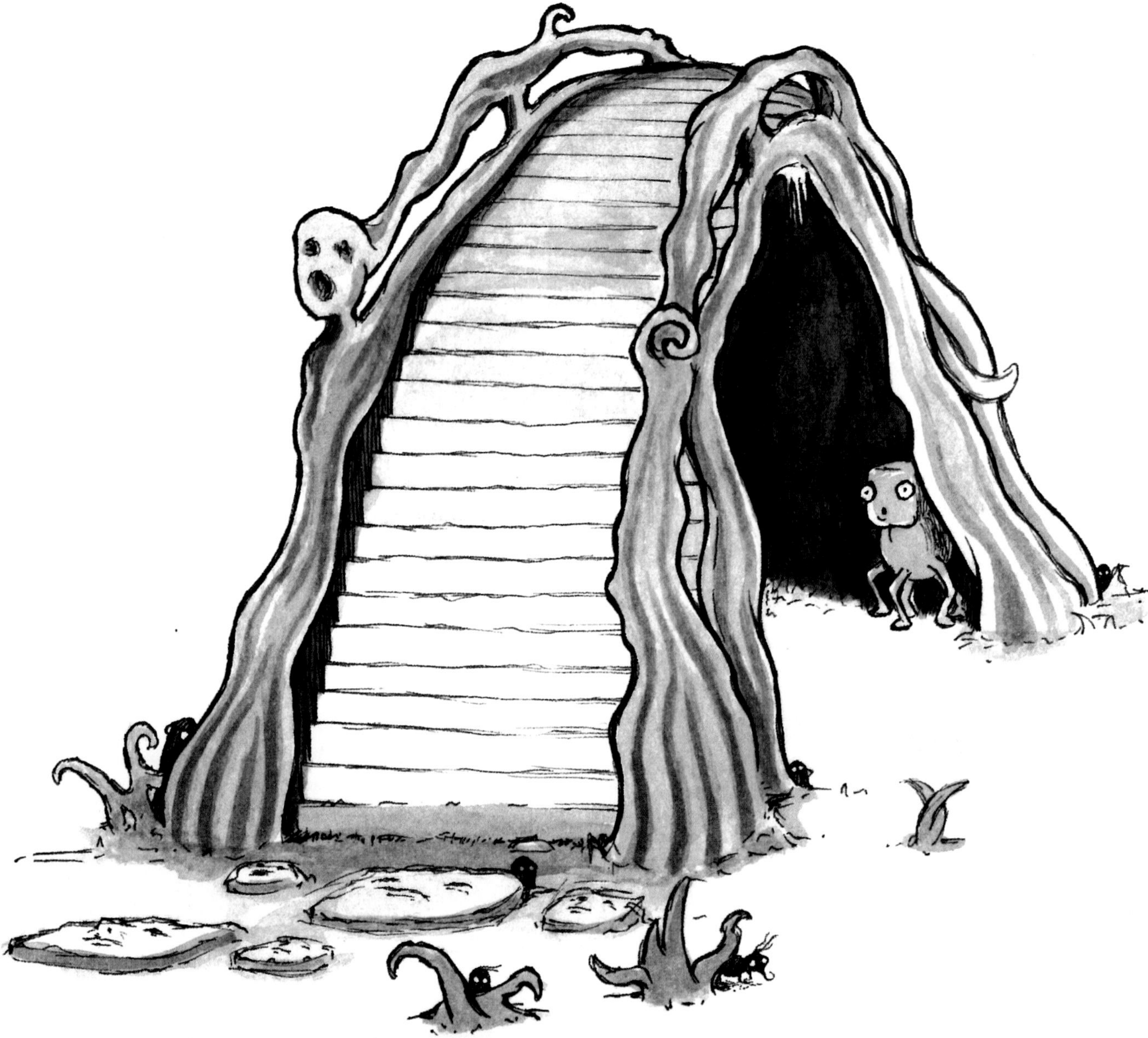

"A bridge," whispered Martha.

"It certainly looks like it," said Sox.

"Nicely polished too," noticed Sheepy, with a craftsman's nod of approval.

"Ahhh, but you're missing the point," said Martha, hands on hips and a glint of, 'I'm much cleverer than you' firmly fixed in the corner of her right eye.

"No water?" said Sheepy.

"Yes, Sheepy!" grinned Sox, proudly, "No water. Well done you. How very, very…"

"Perceptive?" suggested Bob.

"Yes, percept-"

"Shhhhhh," shushed Martha, "what's that?"

Who goes there?

There on a rock beside the bridge was a wizened old tree-stomper.
No taller than a mushroom and about the same girth as a conker in full shine.

"Do you think he's seen us?" whispered Sox, raising his bow and unsheathing an arrow from his quiver.

"Urm, you do know that you've got about a cat in a cupboard's chance of firing that thing?" nodded Martha towards Sox's bow and arrow.

"Shhhh," hushed Sheepy, "he's a bit sensitive about the lack of string."

"Oh," whispered Martha, "fair enough."

Quick as a flash, the tree-stomper scampered on all fours off the rock and on to the bridge, whereupon it stood nonchalantly leaning against the wooden rail, arms crossed and head raised in a distinctly cocky fashion.

"It's seen us," whispered Sox.

"Yup," agreed Sheepy.

"Sure has," nodded Martha.

"Where are we?" said Bob, squinting in the midday sunshine.

"Just about to come into contact with a tree-stomper," smiled Sheepy as Bob shook his flick of hair from one side of his head to the other.

"Oh wow, my grandpop told me about tree-stompers, I think. Could have been tree-slumpers but I'm sure it was stomp not slump." Bob hovered quietly on his umbrella, just above the soft mossy ground.

"What did he say they're like Bob?" asked Sox, holding his stringless bow by his side and re-sheathing his arrow in its quiver.

"Well, it's either an incredibly peaceful and friendly creature with a big heart and timid nature or an ultra aggressive, arrogant and territorial beast which should be avoided at all costs," Bob said, rubbing his chin thoughtfully.

"Hmm," said Sheepy, "what should we do?"

"Oi, what are you waiting for? Are you crossing or not?" called out the tree-stomper from the bridge.

"I've got riddles to guess," the tree-stomper continued, "and painful consequences for failure."

There was a pinch of silence as the friends shuffled boots and looked skywards whilst they semi-ignored the gravelly cry from a few yards yonder.

Finally Sheepy called back, "Urm, we're just having a think about it."

"Well don't take all day, will you? I've got other things to do you know other than bridge-guarding!"

"Ok, will do," called back Sox.

Just then there was a zipping sound and Mouse's head appeared from over Sheepy's shoulder.

"All ok chaps?" Mouse asked, before turning his attention to the bridge situation.

"Ooooh, that's a tree-stomper, isn't it? Frightful creatures, very shouty and not in the slightest bit interested in public spirit or general sensitivity," Mouse shuddered.

"Yeah, that was it!" said Bob, smiling, "Grandpops said that it was tree-stompers that were mean and tree-slumpers that were, like, not mean."

"Oh yes, tree-slumpers are a completely different kettle of elephants. Lovely creatures. Quite wonderful," agreed Mouse, smiling and twisting his upper lip lining.

"Come on then, are you coming over or what?" goaded the gnarled old tree-stomper.

"Anyway, just thought I'd check," said Mouse with a wink before he ducked down and zipped himself safely back into Sheepy's rucksack.

"Well, what shall we do?" spat Martha impatiently, "Who's up for rushing him?"

"Hmm," said Sox, Sheepy and Bob together.

"Come on boys! If we all run at once he'll only be able to take a bite out of one or two of us, which leaves the rest of us free to continue the adventure. Sound good?" Martha stood with her hands on her hips and eyebrows arched so intently that they stretched all the way back to the nape of her neck.

"Hmmmm," was the sum of the group reply.

"What are you waiting for!?" yelled the tree-stomper, "The Big Freeze!?"

"What shall we do?" sighed Sheepy.

"He does look awfully angry," sniffed Sox.

"Yuth couldth alwayth goth aroundth theth bridgeth?" said the muffled voice of Mouse from inside Sheepy's rucksack.

"What was that, Mouse?" asked Sheepy, unzipping the bag from over his shoulder.

"I said," said Mouse, "you could always go around the bridge and thus avoid any kind of altercation with the old tree-stompy type creature."

It took a couple of moments for the alternative idea to sink in but, when it had, it quickly manifested into a work of great significance and even Martha had to agree that it was probably better than sacrificing one, two or more of the adventurers to the fangs of the tree-stomper.

With that, Sheepy, Sox, Martha and Bob began to set off in a right-hand arc so as to meet up with the footpath at a later date whilst also bypassing the bridge and its shouty guardian.

"Oi! What do you think you're doing?" gnashed the angry tree-stomper.

"Urm, nothing," said Sheepy, whilst keeping his eyes firmly fixed in front.

"Oh come on! That's not fair!" cried the tree-stomper, stomping his hairy foot on the bridge.

"Sorry," called out Sheepy, "you have a very nice bridge by the way."

"Oh, thanks very much!" shouted the tree-stomper.

"No problem," called out Sheepy.

"What a nice fella," said Bob.

"Lovely," smiled Sox.

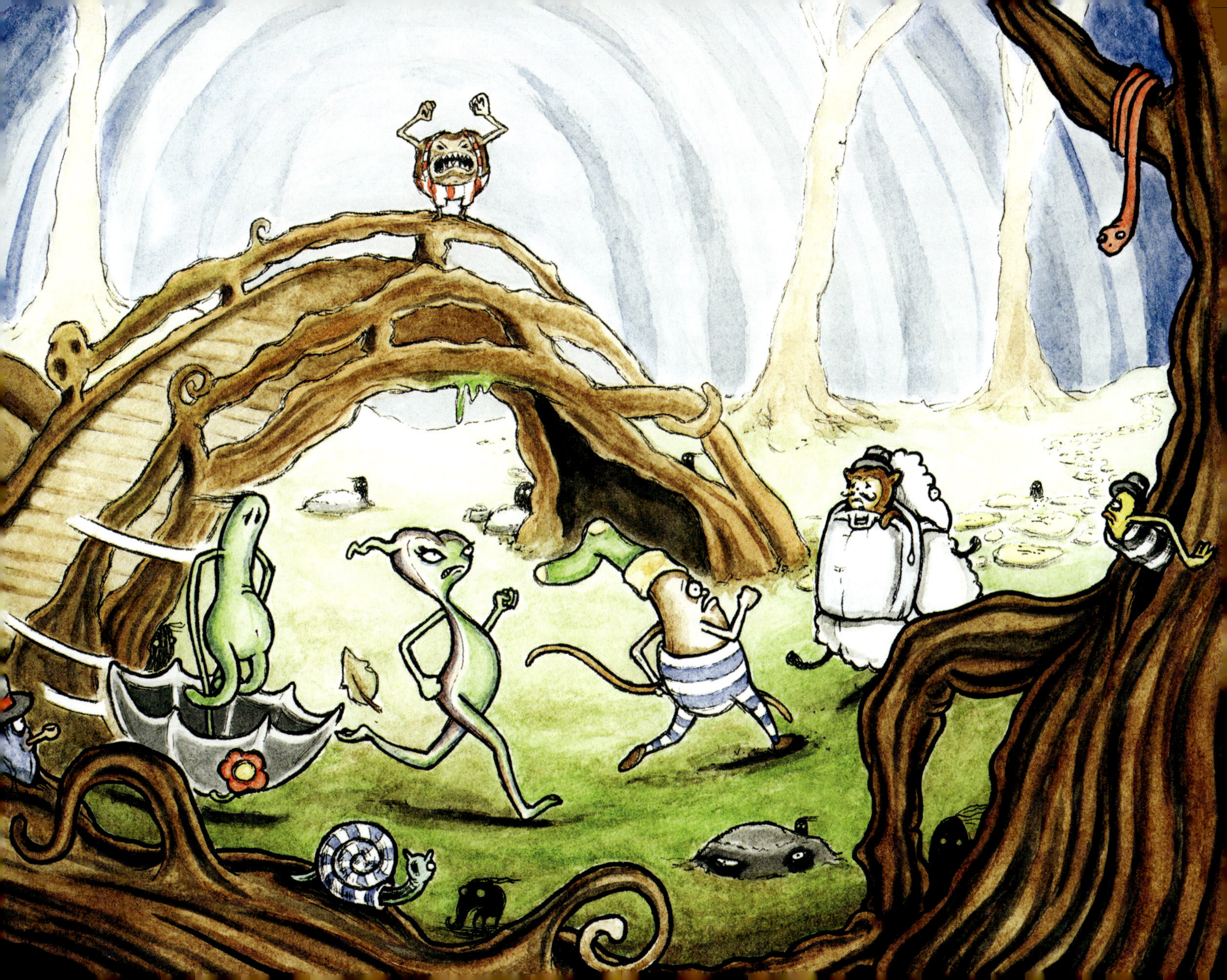

Martha grimaced and shook her head before leading the group onwards, upwards and away from the bridge.

"I was being sarcastic!" yelled the angry tree-stomper, even though anyone who would care to listen was pretty much out of earshot.

The tree-stomper continued to mumble inaudible expletives until the group had disappeared into the distance, whereupon he sat down cross-legged and proceeded to pick at a knothole that had just begun to develop on the cap of his left knee.

"Grrrr," he said to himself, gruffly.

Something Chilly This Way Comes

After all the excitement of negotiating their way past the tree-stomper, the band of merry adventurers proceeded along the path with a particularly upbeat spring in their steps.

In fact, the mood in the camp was so bright and breezy that they barely noticed a dark and foreboding cloud that had decided to edge its way closer to the glowing ball in the sky.

Without even waiting to be introduced the black cloud covered the glowing ball and, in so doing, turned what had been a rather lovely afternoon into a jolly chilly, not-very-nice-to-be-outside kind of early evening.

"Isss annyoonnee feeellliinnggg a llitttllee bitt chilllyyyy?" shivered Bob, as he attempted to run his fingers through his side-parted plop of hair.

"Nnooowww yoou coommmeee toooo meennttttiiioonn itttt," stammered Sox.

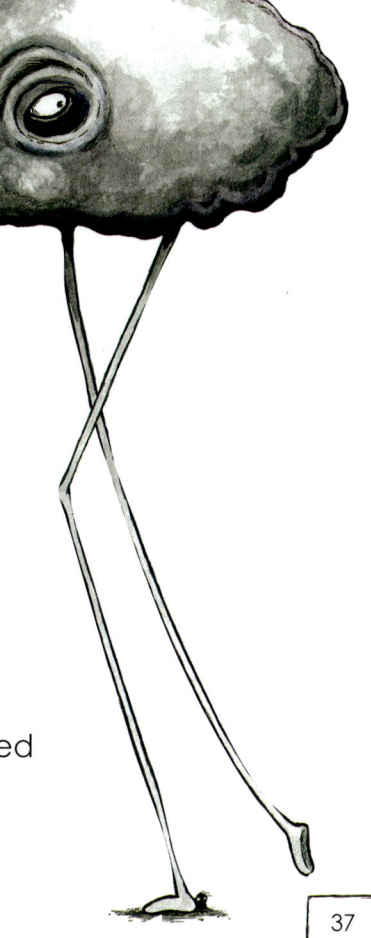

"Ppppeeerrrhhhaappps weee sshhhooulld loook fooooorr shheellter," suggested Martha through gritted teeth and even more gritted toenails.

"Good idea, Martha," smiled Sheepy.

Sheepy's wonderfully warm reply caused everyone to turn their frozen faces towards him in order to ascertain just why there was a distinct lack of shiver in his voice.

"What?" said Sheepy, "Have I got grass in my teeth?"

Sheepy proceeded to have a pick and a pull at his teeth in the hope of removing whatever it was that was causing his face to have suddenly become such compelling viewing.

"Arrrreeey yooouuu nootttt cooolldd, Sheeeeepppppyyy?" Sox just about managed to propel from his fast-freezing vocal chords.

"Cold? Me? No sir. I'm as warm as toast," Sheepy did a little shoulder shrug just to prove how inconsequential the cold actually was to him and, in so doing, he pretty much quadrupled his cuddle value in one fell swoop.

"Easy everyone," laughed Sheepy, "there's plenty of me to go around."

"Yeesss butttt youuu'rrree sooooo waaaarmmm," mumbled Bob through a face full of Sheepy's woolly coat, as the friends gathered round him.

"Hey, what's going on here?" Mouse appeared from out of Sheepy's backpack and immediately nipped back in again only to return seconds later with a pair of earmuffs and a tiny knitted moustache scarf.

"Bit chilly eh, chaps?" said Mouse, his teeth just about holding back a chatter, "Time we found some ssshhhhellltttteeerrr."

Everyone nodded from their hugging spot around Sheepy's waist and began edging forwards. Martha was walking backwards, Sox did a sort of sidestep whilst Bob brought up the rear by clinging to Sheepy's woolly bottom as though he was reading a map in the dark without his glasses.

"There, look, there's somewhere," Sheepy pointed, just as the gathering gloom above let loose an echoing rumble of thunder and the first tip-taps of rain began to appear on the ground.

"Quiiiickly everyoooone," cried Sox, "ttttto the somewheeeeere."

Whether the Wizzle be Wizzle

Without waiting for further instruction, Sheepy heaved himself, Sox, Bob and Martha in the general direction of what appeared to be a medium-sized hole along the verge at the side of the path.

No sooner had they reached the hole, lightning struck and sent a crackling burst of energy hurtling towards the ground.

"Oh wow," said Bob, "that was a big one."

Everyone nodded in agreement as they slowly started to prise themselves from Sheepy's warm and woolly fleece.

"Hey, my teeth have stopped chattering," smiled Bob, "it's pretty cosy in here."

"Mmm, snug," agreed Sox as he sat down on the soft, sandy floor of the hole and watched as rain drops the size of lemons splatted and sploshed against the ground outside.

"I'm not sure I like it," said Martha, sniffing the warm air.

"Oh come on, Martha. This is a lovely hole," said Sox as he watched puddles starting to form.

"Hmmm, I don't know, it just seems a little bit too, well, wizzelly for my liking."

Martha, of course, was right. Inside the warm, medium-sized hole, unbeknown to the group of chilly shelterers, lived a wizzle.

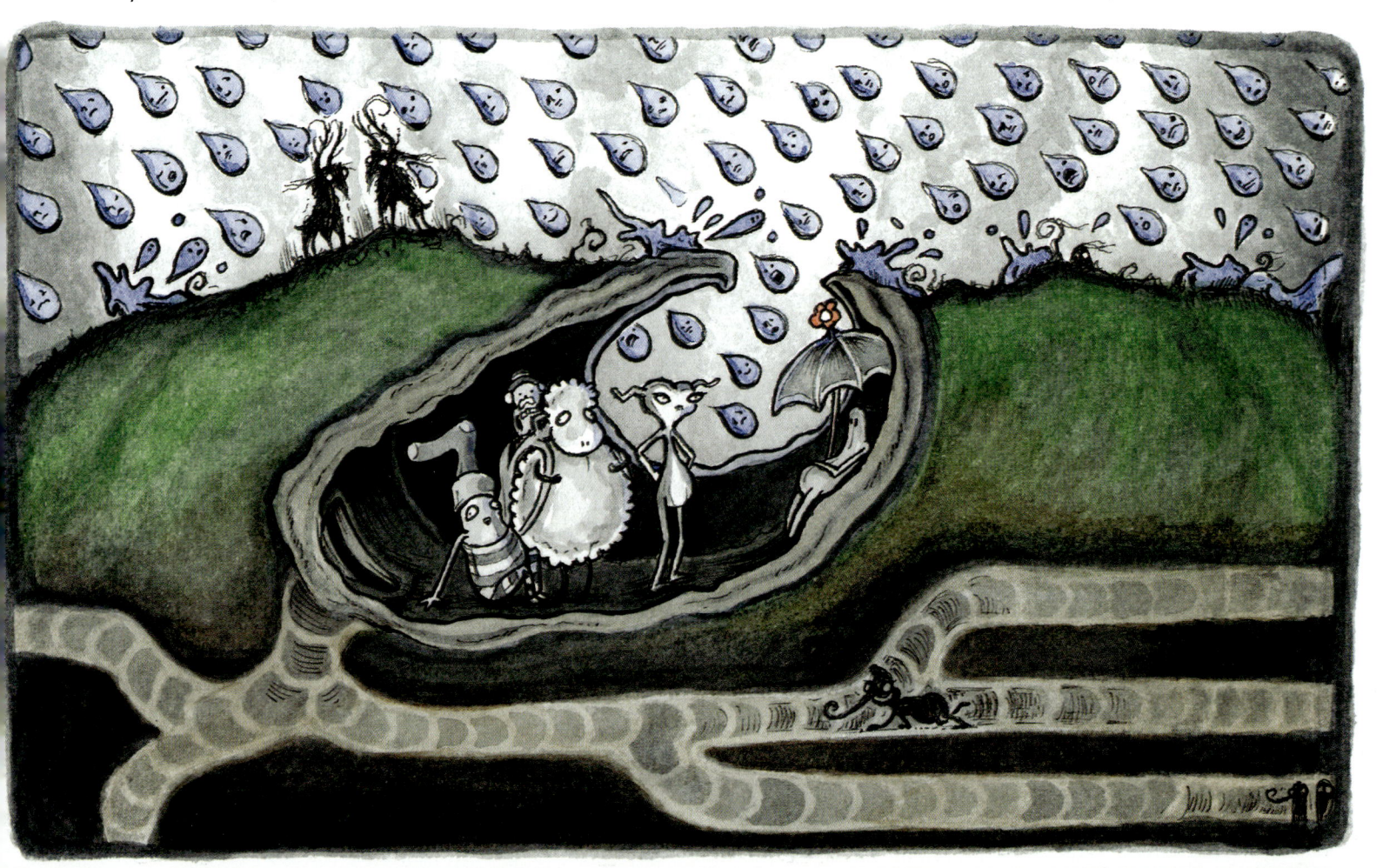

Wizzle by name and wizzle by nature, as the saying goes, and it wasn't long before said wizzle was sniffing and snuffling around its house guests with all the grace and charm of an elderly relative at Christmas.

"Did you just hear something?" asked Martha, still refusing to sit down.

"What sort of something?" replied Sheepy quietly.

"Urm, I don't know really," said Martha, turning to look into the darkness behind her. "It just felt like something was sniffing around my ear."

"Oh, that's odd," nodded Sheepy, his eyes gleaming through the gloom like two large pickled eggs.

"Hey, what was that?" Sox jumped to his feet and backed away against the side of the hole.

"Wow, like, I felt something too," shivered Bob.

"I told you I didn't like this place!" said Martha as she edged her way over to join the others.

The wizzle continued to sniff and snuff its long thin nose up and down each member of the group without ever once considering the need for personal space.

Of course, as wizzles are completely invisible and as blind as buttons, personal space is not usually paramount in their thinking. This particular wizzle had seventy-four hungry offspring to feed, so it was thinking less about social niceties and more about which guest to bite first.

"Ooowwwwwwww!!" yelled Sox as the wizzle made its mind up, "*Wizzle!*"

As one collective mass, Sox, Sheepy, Martha and Bob lunged towards the exit with nothing else on their minds other than avoiding a nasty nip.

It was at that exact same moment that a bolt of lightning decided to shoot down causing the group to stop in their tracks as they found themselves caught between a shock and a hard face.

"What shall we do?!" panicked Sox, trying to protect himself from the wizzle's razor-sharp teeth.

"Where is it? Where's the wizzle?" shouted Martha, swinging her legs and arms about like an out of control Ninja windmill.

"Ouch!" yelled Sheepy.

"Have you got it, Sheepy?" shouted Martha, cart-wheeling her fists in Sheepy's general direction.

"Urm, not really!" cried Sheepy, "But I think it's quite taken a fancy to my stick-like ankles!"

"Ow!" shouted Sheepy as he received a whack in the flanks from Martha's flailing fist.

"Oops, sorry Sheepy, was that you?" apologised Martha before she begun blindly punching in another direction.

"Ouch!" yelped Sox.

"Sorry, Sox," said Martha.

"Stop hitting things Martha, you're worse than the wizzle!" shouted Sox.

"I was just trying to…"

Martha didn't have time to complete her explanation as to why she'd just whacked two of her travelling chums as from out of nowhere a glowing light appeared which completely illuminated the hole.

"Anyone order assistance!" called out Mouse as he held a brightly burning birthday candle above his head.

As soon as the candle light illuminated the wizzle's lair, it retreated as swiftly as it had arrived, leaving Sox and Sheepy rubbing their wounds, several of which had actually been incurred via Martha.

"Mouse, you saved us!" cried Bob, unfolding himself from his umbrella.

"You're a hero, Mouse!" smiled Sheepy.

"Think nothing of it, I'm sure you'd have all done the same for me if you were housed within a bottomless backpack filled with goodness only knows what plus plenty more besides."

"Hmm, good point," said Sox as he stroked his nipped ankles and looked around nervously for any more signs of the hungry wizzle.

"We'd better get going before she comes back for more," sighed Mouse. "Wizzles are notoriously relentless and she's probably got a nest full of babies to feed."

"Ah, you think so?" said Bob quietly.

"Probably, Bob, probably," said Mouse still holding the flickering candle flame aloft.

"Look, it's stopped raining!" shouted Martha from the entrance to the wizzle's lair, "Let's get out of here."

"Good idea," everyone agreed.

Quickly, they all bundled out of the dark, medium-sized wizzle hole and rubbed their eyes in the light that was attempting to project itself from behind the slowly retreating storm cloud.

Large globules of rain hung from trees and bushes, testing gravity for all its faults, before deciding whether or not to hit the muddy ground below and end up as just another drip in a puddle.

Whilst watching one of the aforementioned raindrops, Bob let out an extraordinary loud and long sigh.

"Hhhhhhhhhhhhhhhhhhhhhhhhh," sighed Bob.

The others turned round to see what on earth Bob was sighing about as it was A. Quite out of character and B. Far more melodic than a sigh has a right to be.

"What's up Bob?" asked Sheepy.

"Yeah, what's with the long, loud and melodious sigh, Bob?" said Sox, as he squeezed his sock-shaped head in order to wring out a modicum of moisture.

"Well, you know. It's just that I can't help thinking that that wizzle was only, like, looking out for her babies and we were, like, sort of invading her home," Bob stood with his back to the group and stared at the dark, medium-sized hole.

Everyone looked on in silence whilst occasionally shuffling their feet and staring at the sky above, which had turned from grey to blue in almost the same amount of time it takes to sew a sailor a new pair of pyjamas.

"What do you think we should do, Bob?" asked Sheepy, joining his friend in staring at the entrance to the wizzle's lair.

"Well, you know Sheepy, we do have a few bits and bobs that she might be able to use." Bob turned to Sheepy, "What do you think?"

It didn't take too long for all the group to nod in agreement with Bob's generous bits and bobs sharing plan and, after a quick rummage, Mouse was able to procure a large leaf's worth of food which was placed carefully in front of the medium-sized hole in the grassy verge.

No sooner had the group turned their backs on the hole and rejoined the path to search for answers, than the leaf containing the bits and bobs was whipped out of sight and into the realm of the mother wizzle and her seventy-four hungry offspring.

An Attempt at Defining the Occurrence

After leaving the wizzle and her, now, not so hungry children behind, our group of happy wanderers strolled in the afternoon sunshine and chatted merrily about ankle bites, bits, bobs and just what it's like to be searching for answers without a care in the world.

Bob was still holding on to the warm glow that he had found in the pit of his stomach and the swoosh of his umbrella dusted against daisies and dandelions as he rode alongside Sheepy, Martha and Sox.

Martha had found a large pointy stick and every so often she would thwack a stone or acorn that had dared to cross her path. Martha's aim was a sight to behold and before long she was able to thwack, double thwack and even triple thwack without even a moment's notice.

'Bzz'

As the group continued to follow the path and the glowing ball in the sky continued to warm their backs, Mouse popped out of Sheepy's rucksack and made an announcement.

"Friends, I have an announcement," he announced.

'Bzzz'

"Ooooh, that sounds good, Mouse," said Sheepy, stopping and looking over his shoulder. "Do you need to be placed gently on to the ground?"

"No thank you, Sheepy, I'll make the announcement from shoulder height if that's all the same to you," said Mouse.

'Bzzzz'

"Right you are then," smiled Sheepy.

"Ahem," Mouse cleared his throat, "It is with great pleasure that I can safely say that I think I'm close to solving the riddle of the occurrence."

'Bzzzzz'

There was a lot of eyebrow raising and head nodding amongst the group, which eventually culminated in quiet awe before Mouse determined the time was just about right to continue.

"Yes, it's basically a swappy-round-the-words sort of riddle and once the words have been swapped around you get a new word from the midst, much like a fiery phoenix rising from deep beneath the bowels of Bigatron," Mouse twizzled his moustache ever so subtly and purred with pleasure.

'Bzzzzzz'

There was silence from within the group and more head nodding before Martha piped up.

"So, what is it then?"

Mouse had almost forgotten his assembled audience and drifted off into a proud and distant daze. "Oh yes, sorry, hmm, I haven't quite worked that bit out yet but I'm pretty sure if you take a look here."

'Bzzzzzzzz'

Mouse disappeared back inside Sheepy's backpack and reappeared with the crumpled piece of tree skin, which had the details of the occurrence hurriedly scribbled upon it.

"Sheepy?" Mouse requested.

'Bzzzzzzzzzzzzzzzzzzzzzzzzz'

Everyone waited patiently as Sheepy placed Mouse gently on the ground and the copy of the occurrence was unscrumpled and laid out before them.

"Now, I was thinking…"

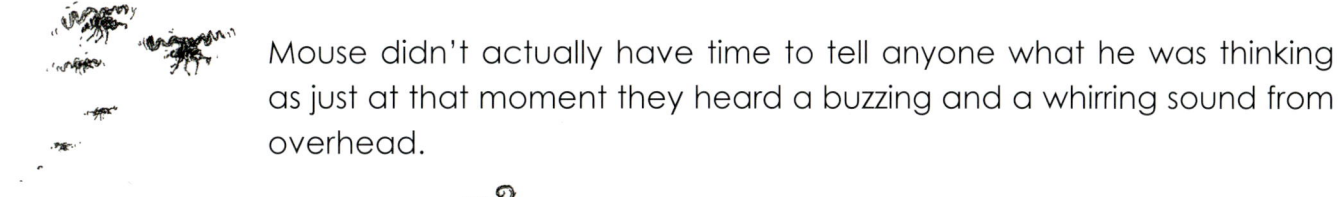

'Bzzzzzzzzzzzzzzzzzzzzzzzzzzzzzzzzzzzzzzzzzzzzzzzzzzzzzz'

Mouse didn't actually have time to tell anyone what he was thinking as just at that moment they heard a buzzing and a whirring sound from overhead.

"Tweedle twitchers!" yelled Martha, swinging her pointy stick around in a vain attempt to attack and protect in equal measure.

'Bzzzzzzzzzzzzzzzzzzzzzzzzzzzzzzzzzzzzzzzzzzzzzzzzzzzzzzzzzzzzzz'

Martha was indeed correct, and as the air filled with flying tweedle twitchers Sheepy and the others began to run with their hands over their heads and fear in their hearts.

One by one each member of the group succumbed to a swooping twitcher and felt a cold clasp on their shoulders before they were carried high into the air.

"This is horrible!" yelled Sox as his tweedle twitcher buzzed close to a dangling Sheepy.

"Not nice at all!" agreed Sheepy, whose little twig-like legs were left blowing in the breeze like shirt tails on a washing line.

"Where are they taking us?" cried Martha, who had dropped her pointy stick in an attempt to fend off her flying assailant.

"Probably back to their nest. Stick this in the bag, Sheepy," shouted Mouse as his tweedle twitcher swooped past in a decidedly upward motion allowing Mouse to thrust the leaf skin copy of the occurrence into Sheepy's outstretched paw.

"*Nest!*" shouted Martha but by then it was too late and already the snap of branches and the twang of leaves was being felt all around as the twiddle twitchers alighted high up in the armpit of a tree where indeed lay their nest and in it, their queen.

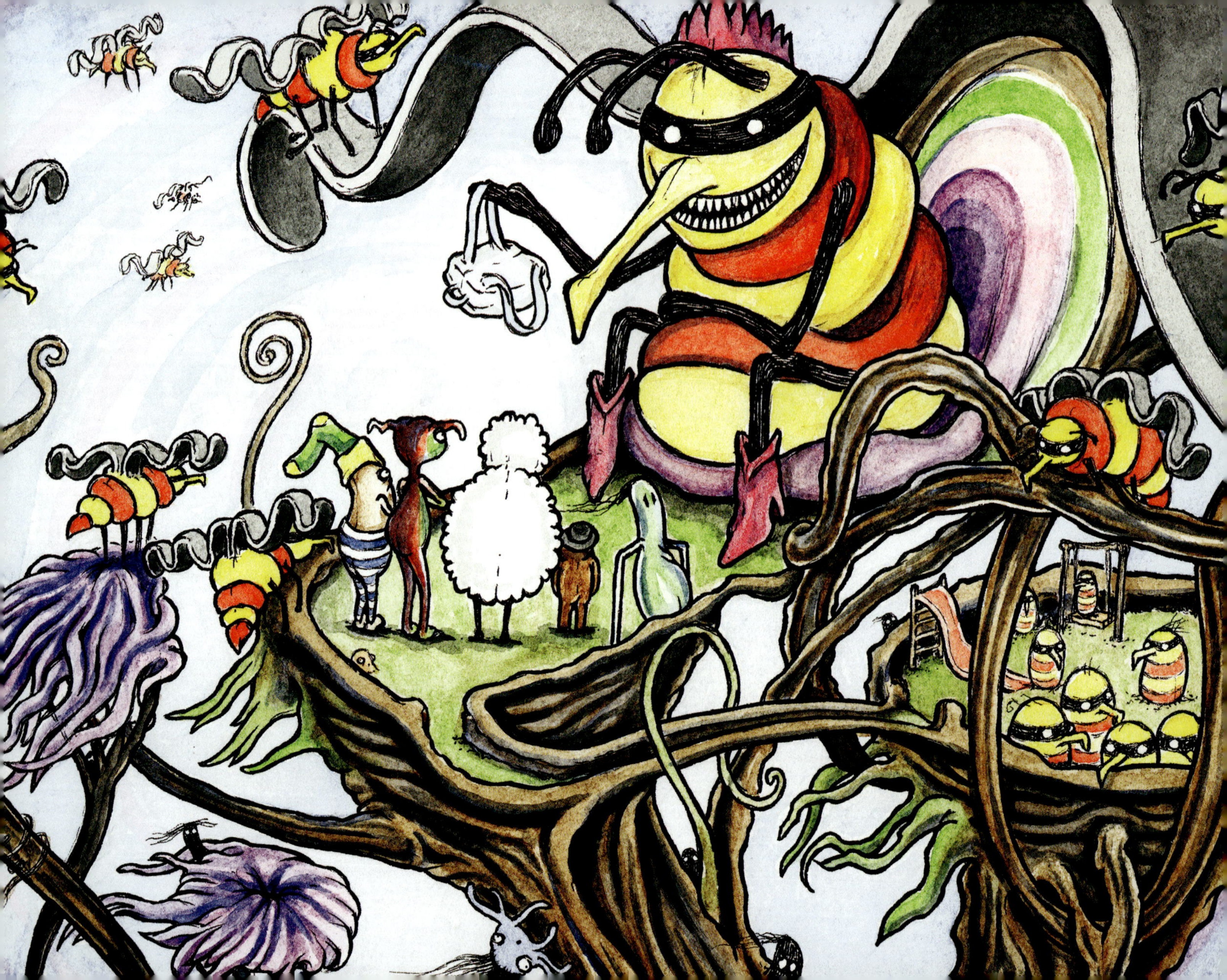

In the Nest of the Tweedle Twitchers

Now, as most normal creatures will no doubt tell you, the trouble with tweedle twitchers is that

1. They're not very bright
2. They're extremely irritatingly buzzy and
3. They will do absolutely anything to please their queen including providing food, shelter and the occasional annoying song around the campfire if deemed appropriate.

Unbeknown to our captured band of once carefree and happy wanderers was that this particular tweedle twitcher queen was, how should one put this, urm, she was a right, yes she was a most, urm, pretty much a…

"Pooooooooo!" shouted the queen, "I need a poooooo!"

As mentioned, tweedle twitchers will do absolutely anything to keep their queen happy including feeding her, washing her and assisting her with other, urm, royal duties.

"What do you think they're going to do to us?" whispered Sox, once the queen was out of sight.

"Not sure," whispered Sheepy.

"What do you think, Mouse?" asked Sheepy to his little moustachioed chum, "What do you think they want with us?"

"Hmm," Mouse rubbed his chin thoughtfully, "they could either be thinking that we want to attack their queen and so they've brought us back to their nest for questioning or…"

"Or what?" hissed Martha, just as the queen returned from her royal duties.

"Silence you horrible little pipsqueaks," buzzed the queen, "there'll be no hissing in my presence."

Martha clenched her fists and bared her teeth but deceased hissing for the time being.

"Right, this is what's going to happen," continued the queen, "first we're going to place you in the Fun Fun Fun Nursery with the infant tweedle twitchers."

"Hey, that doesn't sound too bad," whispered Bob under his breath.

"And then we're going to watch the infant tweedle twitchers eat you!" spat the queen.

"Oh no!" said Bob, "That does sound bad."

"Hmm, yes, that was the other thing," nodded Mouse sagely.

"Any last requests?" added the queen politely.

The group sat in stunned silence as tweedle twitchers buzzed around the queen and made a nuisance of themselves by generally being very buzzy and annoying.

"Hey, that's my bag!" cried Sheepy as a couple of large brutes hoisted up Sheepy's ruck-sack and carried it between them high above the nest.

"Bring it to me!" shouted the queen angrily.

Sheepy and his friends watched helplessly as the two large tweedle twitchers buzzed back down and deposited Sheepy's rucksack in front of the queen.

"What's inside this dirty pocket?" snarled the queen.

Everyone looked at Mouse who had gone slightly red in the cheeks and whose moustache had started to twitch as if it were alive.

"Well," started Sheepy, "we did have a few bits and bobs but we gave them to a hungry wizzle and now…"

"Yes?" screeched the queen impatiently.

"Well now, I guess, we've just got a tree skin copy of an occurrence and a load of nonsense." Sheepy shrugged his shoulders at what amounted to the sum contents of his backpack.

"A load of what?" said the queen curiously.

"Nonsense maam, a load of nonsense, let me show you," said Sheepy stepping forward.

The guards immediately buzzed at Sheepy, stopping him in his tracks.

"Let him through guards," smiled the queen, "let this bundle of fluff show us his nonsense before we feed him to the infants."

The guards buzzed out of the way in a very annoying fashion and allowed Sheepy to walk over to the queen and undo the folds of his rucksack that had, admittedly, become very dirty.

Everyone watched with bated breath as Sheepy delved and rummaged before pulling out a withered brown leaf that appeared to be packed-full of something or other.

"Open it, fluffy," said the queen.

Sheepy, not being one to not do as he was told, did exactly what he was told and unwrapped the nonsense from its leafy covering.

Inside the leaf parcel sat a small brown lump of nonsense.

"Well!" roared the queen, "What does it do?"

"Urm, not sure really," said Sheepy a bit, well, sheepishly.

"We've been had!" mumbled Martha.

"Guards!" screamed the queen, "Take them to the Fun Fun Fun Nursery. It's time for tea!"

With that, the queen threw the small brown lump of nonsense out of the nest and over the side of the tree, whereupon it tumbled off branches and over bark until it landed slap bang on the ground far, far below.

High up above the discarded lump of nonsense, hundreds of irritatingly excited tweedle twitchers swarmed all over the nest and grabbed hold of our condemned adventurers.

"Get off me!" shouted Martha as tweedle twitchers clasped her arms and legs.

"Hey that nips a bit you know!" said Bob as a couple of twitchers pinched his green skin as they began to drag him away.

"Oh Sheepy," called out Sox, "is this how it ends?"

"I certainly hope not Sox, I certainly hope…"

"Look!" cried Mouse, "Look!"

Down below the tweedle twitchers' nest something round and red was beginning to rise.

At first the tweedle twitchers took very little notice of the round, red and rising thing but it wasn't long before first one, then another and then all of them noticed and acted accordingly by screaming and screeching in the most annoying fashion.

"Hold firm you idiots, hold firm!" yelled the queen as several burly looking guards carried her above their heads in order to get her to safety.

"What," gasped Martha, "is that?"

A cracking and a creaking sound echoed throughout the lower, middle and then the upper branches of the tree as the round, red rising thing continued on its ascent with no sign of stopping.

"Get them!" yelled the queen from above the heads of her guards but it was every tweedle twitcher for itself as they ran for cover and forgot all about their baby-feeding prisoners.

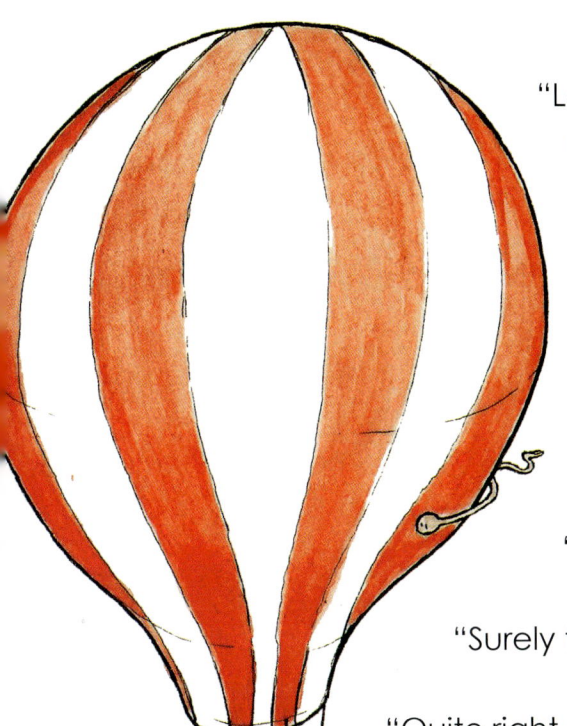

"Looks to me like an escape," shouted Mouse as the red, round rising thing twanged and thwacked a few large branches to one side, catapulting at least a dozen tweedle twitchers in the process.

"When I say jump, jump," cried Mouse above the annoying din of screaming tweedle twitchers.

"What is it?!" shouted Sox.

"No idea!" yelled Sheepy.

"Surely this is just nonsense!" shouted Martha.

"Quite right Martha, quite right! Now one, two, three, JUMP!" cried Mouse, just as the red, round rising thing began to pull away from the tree's branches to reveal a rather well placed wicker basket that was dangling beneath its fiery belly.

The gigantic red balloon continued to pull free of the tree's branches as the five gallant friends leapt from the tweedle twitchers' nest and landed safely into the warm wicker basket being towed underneath.

"It's a hot air balloon!" laughed Martha.

"It sure is!" smiled Sheepy as the balloon rose above the tops of the trees and sailed effortlessly on the late afternoon breeze.

Left behind by the flying friends, the queen tweedle twitcher hopped and cursed and shook her fist in redundant rage as the giant red balloon floated higher and higher before finally disappearing out of sight.

"That was a close one!" said Bob whilst checking the folds of his umbrella for damage.

"It sure was," agreed Sox, "urm, is anyone else up for more adventures?"

All that could be heard was the gentle hum of the fire that continued to power the red, round and rising balloon and, as silence turned to sighs and then to sniggers and finally to laughs, hoots and guffaws, the friends all knew that it was time to head home.

A Call For Answers

As the late afternoon breeze continued to rustle through the leaves of the trees, a flag was hoisted aloft and a bugler held a severed acorn to his lips and started to bugle.

Silence fell over the glade as two mites lifted the chief on to his throne and waited for the ceremonial sneeze to signal the start of procedures.

"*Aaaaatttccchhhhoooooooooo*," sneezed the chief and promptly fell backwards on his throne prior to dabbing delicately at his bulbous cranberry-coloured snout.

"You can talk now," issued the chief as he settled his large feet atop of two willow slugs and held his hands in his large and comfortable lap.

"Oh, hang on!" ordered the chief, committing the glade to silence.

"Bring forth the occurrence would you?" he beckoned to a council member who had been waiting nervously in the wings.

"Ahem, you can talk again," coughed the chief.

Amidst a general din of chitchat and chirruping, the glade council member came forth to the stage dragging the rather neatly folded piece of lined paper which had commonly begun to be referred to as 'the occurrence'.

The general hubbub slowly began to desist as the council member unfolded the occurrence and laid it out flat in front of the chief, whereupon a troupe of mites streamed forth and held the occurrence upright whilst in what can only be described as a pyramid position.

"Very good," said the chief to one of the mites at the base of the pyramid, "very good."

"Thank you, sir. *Arrghh*," grimaced the mite as one of the mites in the second tier trod on his antenna.

"Now," started the chief, as he walked around to the front of the occurrence, "as you all know, some time ago, possibly this morning, I asked for answers."

There was a hushed cloud of whispers that hung over the crowd, like steam off of ice cream as it exits the freezer.

"Well then," continued the chief, "do we have any?"

The cloud of whispers slowly and quietly disappeared until all that remained was an eerie hush and the faraway chirping of a cricket who was returning home after a good day's cricketing.

"Anyone?" asked the chief, raising his eyebrows and placing his hands on his hips.

"*Anyone*?" he said again, but a lot louder, just in case no one had heard him the first time.

"Urm," piped up a brave young pip in the front row.

"Ah, yes young pip," beamed down the chief, "what answers do you have to offer?"

"Urm, please can I go to the toilet?" said the pip quietly.

The chief sighed a loud and prolonged sigh as the pip was taken by the hand and led to the toilet by its mother.

"Does nobody have any answers for me?" the chief asked one more time.

Just then there was an incredible cracking sound:

'Ccrraxxxkkkrrrraaaaaaaaaaaaacccccccccckkkkkkkkkkkkkkkkkkkkk'

"What is it?"

"The sky is falling down!"

"We're all doomed!"

"It's a thresher, it's a thresher!"

"Run for your lives!"

Screams, squawks, squeals and squeaks emitted from the glade as pips, urchins, rumples and luggles ran hither and dither in order to escape the thing from above that may or may not be a thresher but was certainly loud and most definitely scary.

"Wait! Wait!" shouted a loud hailer from high up above, "It's all right, it's only us."

"Us? Us? Who or what is an Us?" shouted the chief as the pyramid of mites finally toppled over backwards, covering the chief with the occurrence in the process.

Finally the scary thing from above stopped snapping branches and bending twigs as it came to rest about a giraffe's neck's distance above the glade.

The general hithering and dithering slowly, but surely, began to abate as it became all the more clear that the sky wasn't about to fall down and something rather special was just about to happen.

"It's us," cried Sheepy from over the side of the swaying basket, "and we have answers."

A stunned and awed hush fell upon the glade as council members and piplings alike looked upwards at the dangling nest and watched open-mouthed as Sheepy was joined at the side of the basket by Sox, Bob and Martha.

"*Is that you, Sheepy?*" called out Mr Shouty, deafening several fripjibbers in the process.

"Yes, it is," bellowed back Sheepy, "we've been on an adventure."

"*An adventure?*" shouted out the shouty council member.

"Yes an–"

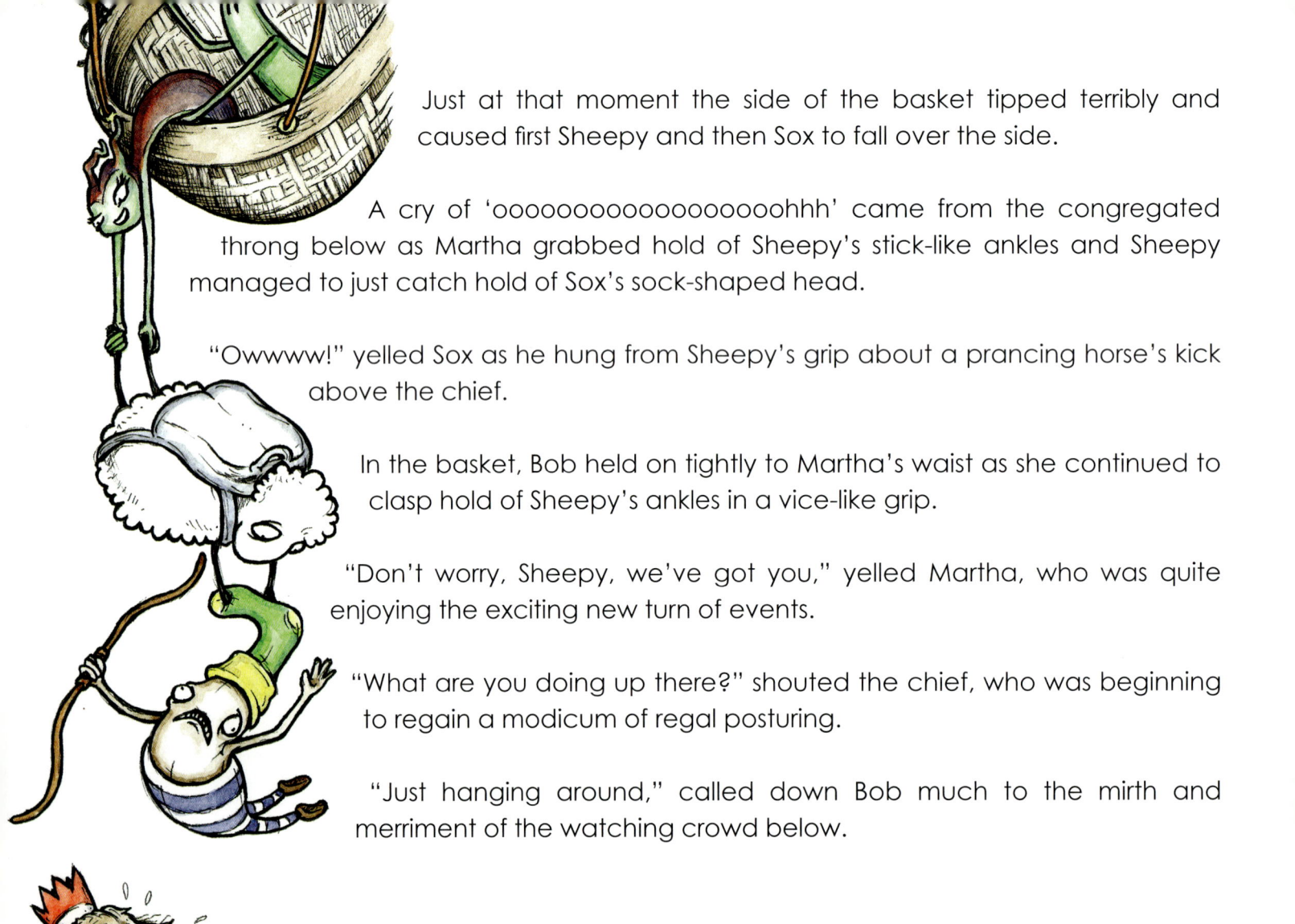

Just at that moment the side of the basket tipped terribly and caused first Sheepy and then Sox to fall over the side.

A cry of 'ooooooooooooooooooohhh' came from the congregated throng below as Martha grabbed hold of Sheepy's stick-like ankles and Sheepy managed to just catch hold of Sox's sock-shaped head.

"Owwww!" yelled Sox as he hung from Sheepy's grip about a prancing horse's kick above the chief.

In the basket, Bob held on tightly to Martha's waist as she continued to clasp hold of Sheepy's ankles in a vice-like grip.

"Don't worry, Sheepy, we've got you," yelled Martha, who was quite enjoying the exciting new turn of events.

"What are you doing up there?" shouted the chief, who was beginning to regain a modicum of regal posturing.

"Just hanging around," called down Bob much to the mirth and merriment of the watching crowd below.

At the precise moment that Bob's carefree quip was being understood by the majority of the gathered glade-dwellers, there was a zipping sound from just behind Sheepy's shoulder blades.

"Your majesty," came a voice from above, "we have your answers."

It was Mouse, of course, appearing from over Sheepy's shoulder. In one hand he clutched a scrumpled piece of tree skin that was scrawled in scribbles, ruminations and doodles and in the other he held on to Sheepy's backpack like a circus performer perched aloft a flying trapeze.

"Hurrah!"

"Woohoo!"

"Wayhey!"

Came a cacophony of voices from down below as the glade-dwellers began to realise that they were off the hook when it came to having to submit answers to the chief.

Mouse waved the scrumpled piece of tree skin and smiled at the crowd.

"I think he's quite enjoying this," said Bob to Martha, who were both still clinging on to their dangling friends like anglers with a 10lb pike.

"Answers have you!" bellowed the chief, "Why didn't you say so."

Sox was also starting to quite enjoy the adulation, and smiled as he swung gently above the chief and waved to the crowd below to further encourage whoops and cheers of delight.

"Come on then acrobats, what are these answers that you talk of?" shouted the chief, which further enticed the crowd to add their own calls.

"Yeah, we want answers!"

"Give us your answers!"

"What am I going to have for my tea?"

"Ahem," Mouse cleared his throat and held his scribbled notes in the air.

"Get on with it, Mouse," called Martha, "my hands are slipping."

"Oh, yes, right you are," said Mouse, as his moustache bristled with excitement.

"We have three answers for you sire," started Mouse.

"Ohhhhhhhhh," the crowd chorused.

"Very good," muttered the chief.

"And the first answer is…ahem," Mouse cleared his throat again as the crowd waited in anticipation.

"If you can't get over it, you can always go around it."

Cheers and applause rang out through the glade.

"Lovely, well done, Mouse," smiled Sheepy, as he readjusted his grip on Sox's head.

"Thank you, Sheepy," mumbled Mouse before continuing.

"The second answer is…" the crowd held their breath.

"One creature's food is another creature's stick-like ankle."

More cheers, hand clapping and fevered whooping made Mouse blush with pleased as punch pride.

"Great show, Mouse, great show," called down Bob as he readjusted his grip on Martha's waist.

"Quickly Mouse," called Martha, "last one."

"Oh yes, and the last answer is…"

The crowd bit their nails. Martha's grip began to slip. Bob lost his footing.

"A little bit of nonsense goes a long way!"

With that, Martha's grip on Sheepy's ankle completely gave way, causing Sheepy, Sox and Mouse to free fall to the ground below where they narrowly managed to avoid hitting the chief but failed to miss Mr Shouty and several other glade council members.

"Marvellous!" yelled the chief, "Marvellous!"

"*Ouch!*" shouted Mr Shouty, "*I dink you squadged my dose!*"

A Lovely, Lovely Banquet

After Martha and Bob had finally managed to get down from the hanging balloon basket and Sheepy, Sox and Mouse had picked themselves up from a pile of council members, the chief patted backs, shook hands and declared a great banquet was to be held in their honour.

That very same evening a huge banqueting table was laid and readied in the glade. It was full of all kinds of goodies and no one was left out when it came to particular dietary requirements and preferred methods of disposal.

The chief, as was the norm for this type of occasion, sat himself at the head of the table and right next to him, in pride of place, sat Sheepy, Sox, Martha, Bob and Mouse with silly smiles slapped right across their happy faces.

Every creature from the world on the hill was invited and found a place around the table, much to the delight of our brave and proud adventurers and much to the displeasure of the busy council members, who had had to swap their clipboards for aprons as they helped distribute the food and fancies.

Sheepy and Mouse took great pleasure in conversing with the chief and explaining just how they'd managed to come up with such wonderful answers and it wasn't long before a great merrymaking singsong had begun involving a pip-organ and several seed-pipes.

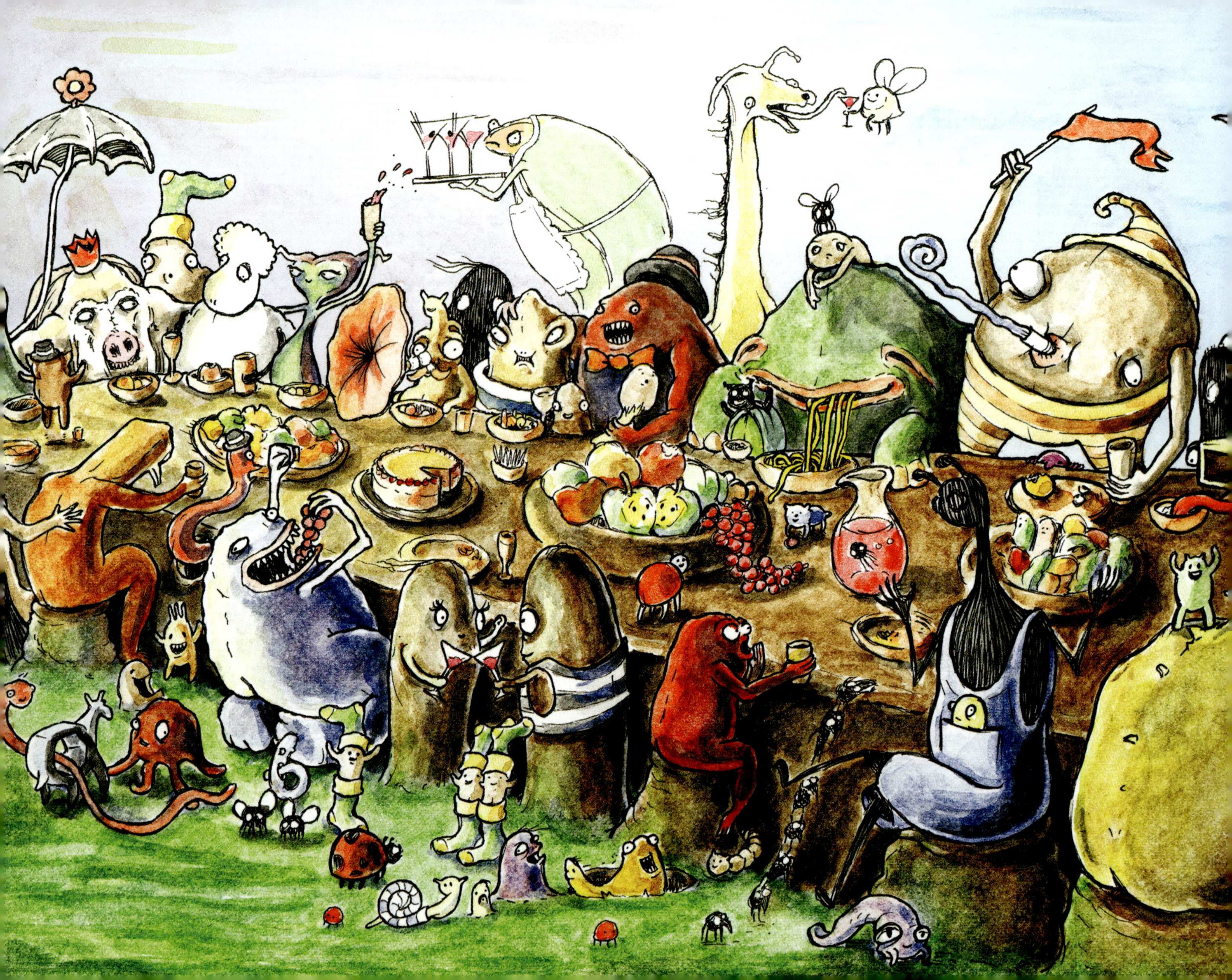

As evening turned to night and night turned to morning, the creatures on the hill finally started to disperse back to their lodgings as the glowing ball in the sky saw them off to bed with a tender kiss to their foreheads and a warm stroke to their backs.

Sox snoozed peacefully in the morning glow of light and nuzzled gratefully into a pillow of moss that had somehow managed to find its way onto his left temple.

Against Sox's sock-shaped head lay Martha, who occasionally twitched and smiled in her sleep as she recounted tales of derring-do and great adventures.

Beside the pair, tucked up neatly in his umbrella, Bob snored wistfully as his dreams led him down flower-festooned paths and over hillsides encrusted with honeycomb sprinkles.

It was only Sheepy and Mouse who hadn't yet succumbed to the sumptuous splendour of slumber and splayed before them lay the cause of their insomnia. Something white and scribbled upon. Something that had caused a quest for answers but also contained an answer in itself.

"So, Mouse," said Sheepy, sleepily, "what you're saying is…"

Sheepy yawned a long and lovely yawn before continuing.

"What you're saying is that there's an answer hidden within this occurrence," Sheepy scratched his bottom and rolled over on to his back to enjoy the first tickles of sunlight that were beginning to peep through the leaves overhead.

"Quite right Sheepy," sniffed Mouse, "I think I've just about cracked it but I might need a little bit of help. Fresh pair of eyes and all that."

"Do you think we should tell the chief?" whispered Sheepy, glancing over to where the chief and a pile of council members lay snoring upon a clump of dandelions.

"No, no, no. No need to wake the big chap, I'm sure we can work it out for ourselves," Mouse tapped his nose and tousled his moustache before flattening out the occurrence on a particularly soft and springy arrangement of lichen.

"Now," began Mouse, "what we need to do is arrange the words in a different order. Once they're arranged differently, a new word will appear. It could well be that the new word is just to be taken from the first letter of each word and thus…"

'Snoooooooooooooooooooooooooooorrrrrrrrrrrrrrrrrrreeeeeeeeeeeeeeeee.'

Sheepy's snores resonated around the glade and caused Mouse to shake with jovial laughter as he folded up the occurrence, rubbed his little eyes and crawled into Sheepy's backpack.

And there we must leave the world on the hill. Slumbering and snoozing peacefully far away from sight and mind.

If you fancy having a crack at the occurrence riddle yourself then please be my guest. If you manage to untangle the answer, then swear to keep it close to your heart until next time we meet as, who knows, you might well be needing it on your own adventures.

I bid you good day and good hunting.

The Riddle

So, young adventurers, this is your chance to visit the World of Sheepy online and submit your occurrence answer to the glade council members who will then pass it on to the chief.

All that's required is a computer or other form of witchcraft portal and the ability to type the following website address: **www.worldofsheepy.com** using your paws or pointy stick.

After successfully negotiating the gateway to the online World of Sheepy, you'll be invited to enter your answer whereupon you'll *unleash the fires of Bigatron!*

Only joking.

Once you've entered the correct answer you'll unlock numerous treasures and hidden Sheepy secrets that may lead to goodness only knows what but definitely not the fires of Bigatron.

Anyway, best of luck with your online quest and thank you very much for visiting *The World of Sheepy*.

Henrietta Williams

Growing up in Wimbledon, Henrietta had a wonderful childhood roaming Wimbledon Common, home of the Wombles, with her friends and little Jack Russell, Smudge. She now has 3 grown-up boys, the eldest of which is responsible for the original Sheepy doodle. Today she lives in Sussex with her husband and two wonderful un-cat-like cats, Mouse and Sunny. Henrietta hopes that The World of Sheepy has created a place where children are encouraged to engage with their imagination and surroundings as she did. This is her first venture into publishing, but she has big plans for Sheepy, so it definitely won't be her last.

Richard Berner

Richard Berner is an artist and illustrator based in Brighton, UK. As well as children's book illustration, Richard specialises in surreal pen drawings and paintings. His highly successful "Beasts of Brighton" series can be viewed on the Berner Designs website, along with other pieces in his unique, imaginative style.

www.bernerdesigns.co.uk

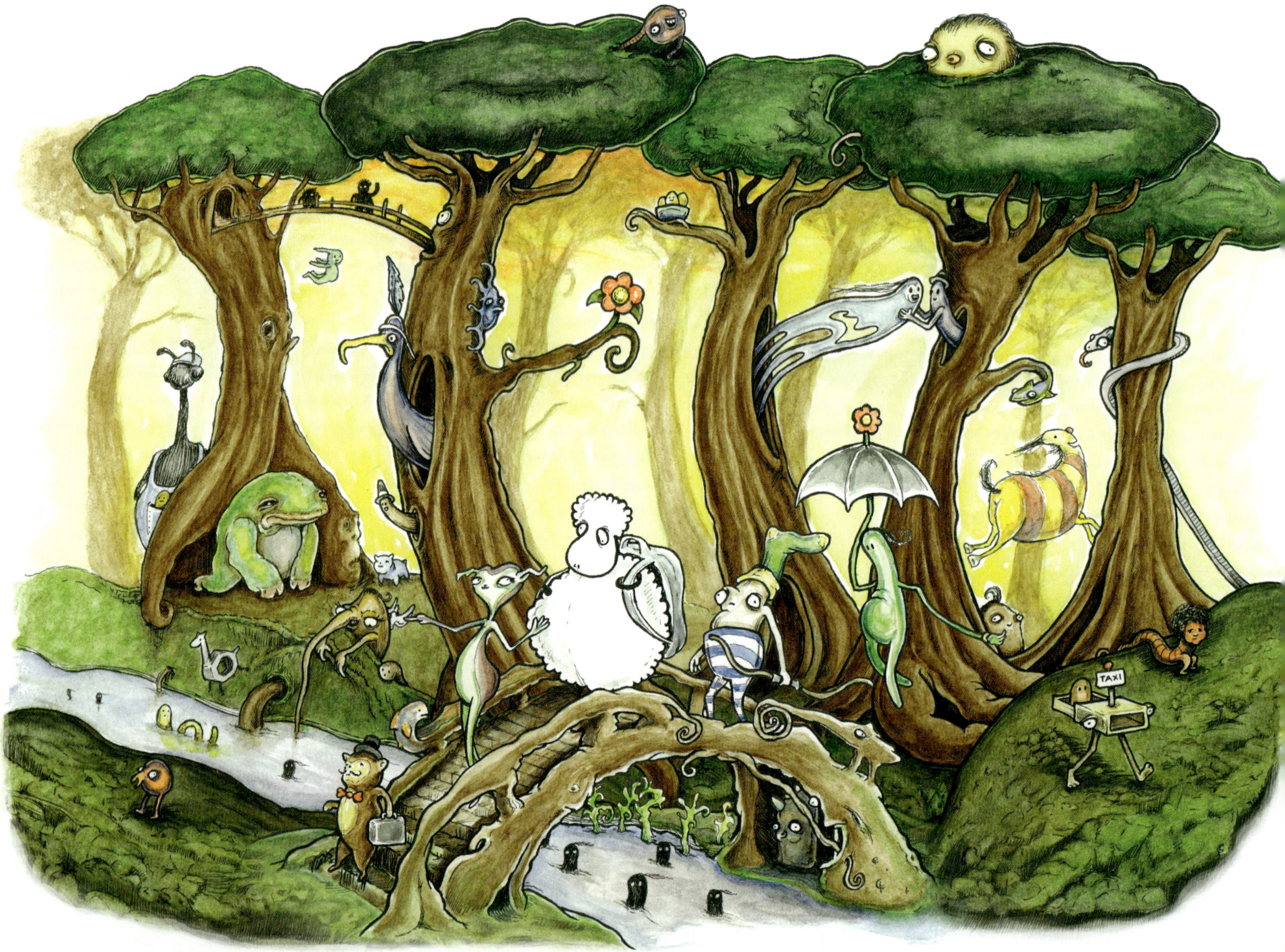
TAXI